Nottingham

Nottingham

Guest-Edited by
Miggy Angel

Dostoyevsky Wannabe Cities

An Imprint of Dostoyevsky Wannabe

First Published in 2019
by Dostoyevsky Wannabe Cities

Dostoyevsky Wannabe Cities is an imprint of
Dostoyevsky Wannabe publishing.

www.dostoyevskywannabe.com

This book is a work of fiction. The names, characters and incidents portrayed in it are the work of the authors' imagination. Any resemblance to actual persons, living or dead, events or localities is entirely coincidental.

Cover design by Dostoyevsky Wannabe Design

ISBN-9781093933604

Dostoyevsky Wannabe Cities books represent a snapshot of the writing of a particular locale at a particular moment in time. The content is reflective of the choices of the guest-editor.

Editor's Note:

"We tried to get Byron, Sillitoe and Lawrence for this collection but it turns out THEY ARE DEAD.

So, here's a diverse selection of fantastic, alive, Nottingham-based writers.

Notts! Bring your writers flowers while they are still alive, don't wait till they're dead."

—Miggy Angel

Contents

Bridie Squires

Sneinton Market

A hardhatted man sings the final countdown,
wraps industrial Christmas lights
around a recently erected tree.

The woman in the cafe says
"She han't been very well"
when he asks about her mam.
Every time she draws out
the caramel tart from the fridge,
chips away at another slice,
she serves it up with a wonky smile.

Volkswagen Golf

Sandstorm steady.
Bass-pump vibrate, home.
Boy racer? No.
Gyal cruiser. Faceless.
Top-half hair-bun lifted
Red light back shifts cool
Through Wilford Grove.

Skirting Board

You're wrapped in a towel
and shower dew, hair flat
with an unsqueezed drip;
he drowning-child holds you.
Ebbing clouds stream in
and out of your iris.
It's been a while since weather like this.
There's damp creeping in-
-to the skirting board;
he unscrews, pokes around,
says he'll *keep an eye on it,* that
we can't be letting it get any worse.

Self Portrait with Sparrows

I've got a stash of sparrows
stored in my arsehole.
Often I feel them, happy and impatient –
swaddling in the jacuzzi of my stomach,
buzzing in the West Indian Centre bass of my heart,
screaming at the DJ to fuck off and pull up.
Sometimes one of them beaks its way out
chirping into the black hole of a man's throat
where it builds a nest and sings
for around a year or so.
Often I wonder why they go there –
there are clifftops in Croatia, and windowsills in
Bangkok
to migrate to. But these little bastards
want blood; the warmth of the choke.
No, they never seem to go very far at all.

Rich Goodson

Monolingual

Queueing queueing queueing at this check-in desk
all these moonymoany britishfuckers
are mono-fucking-lingual! Gatwick-bound?
We do hope your ticket's single. Because,
old chap, though we legions of profligate
babblers, heathen bunglers, can go private
in multitudinous linguistic jungles,
we can also see through your every word.

Your holy gift has become your come-uppance.
What? Nowhere to hide? We don't give a tuppence!
Bon voyage! Buon viaggio! Rehlat saeida!
Soon you'll be swaddled in aeroplanes home:
glass babies

                        white-hot from the womb. The sun

slants through them

                        midwives wipe them

                                like vases.

When Do We Say 'I Do'?

In the mosque? In the synagogue? In the church?
In a bridal gown? A suit?

Or up here naked on an outhouse roof in southwest
France
on a Saturday night / Sunday morning, in July,
around 1a.m.?

As the moon mimics a human ear
pressed up against us, so close we can stroke the
hairs along its lobe?

Or when I clown about:
Take my hand in holy   animal   husbandry!

Or when – serious – the night feels like the hold of
a warplane
musky with horses, their eye-whites stars?

Or when all this crashes down into the lavender, the
rosemary, the sage
into the fireflies, into the transfused poppies – is that
when?

Or when our bodies combust, under the smoke, out
in the field

in the centre of this stillness – is that when?

Or after? As we get dressed
sorting out whose are whose in the moon's ash?

Everything's granular. Greying.
& in English? French? Latin? Hebrew? Arabic?
Or Sanskrit?

That cast-iron Jesus at the edge of the maize-field
hangs
his thighs jazzed with rust.

The sunflowers are fidgeting to a music only they
can hear.
It's a pass-the-parcel game: Dawn is being passed
down the rows.

We can see it: rows upon rows of sunflowers pausing
to unwrap it
blood coming back to their faces

something jade, something cadmium
something new.

& they're passing it up to us. Stop! Our turn!
We unwrap Dawn into our eyes.

Onto our skin. Onto our tongue.
Into a quinine   tang   of air.

Lightning Sutra

There's a space under the pulmonary aorta   left
of the   right of the   brain. Like
that rock-shrine under Nottingham Castle, sealed in
1535, where an alabaster Virgin weeps tears which
may or may not, which may or may not, be milk.

There's a gorge between the hemispheres of the
brain   left of the   right of the   pelvis. A
vacuum, a silence, like that snow-cave in Annapurna.
The last Yeti sat at the entrance to it & chanted a
sutra.

There's a grotto even Freud can't reach, where you
run out of the words to cure yourself. You spin the
same old story till the point of it wears a hole in
your tearduct, in your pants, in your universe.
You're like a spider, creeping near the unplugged
plughole, near the vortex of squealing water.

Call it the vertigo of Subatomic Space. Or the
indigo of Deep Space. Or Emptiness. Or Cat-Got-
Your-Tongue. Or the freefall as you step off the
precipice, the edge of the delusion of You. To the
place which is no-place, which is blankspace.

Lightning once cracked out of it   left of

my   right of my

Don't even think of politics, or ethics, or religion, till you've knelt like a blubbering child at the edge of it & paid your dues.

Andrew Graves

Nylon Flights Of Fancy

When me and our Martyn were boys
mam gave us butterfly catchers
fashioned out of garden canes,
hoops of wire
and the legs of old American tan tights.
They became our favourite summertime tools.

Homemade dream snatchers.

Together we swept the neighbour's heaving
     buddleia,
excitedly laddering the sky
with our little nets of joy
that fluttered with proud childishness

and dancing powder-blushed
captured wings.

Anne Holloway

City Songs

In the city men in bright jackets
sweep the streets for stars,
rake the canal to catch the moon
and drop it in a bucket.
Women hum under their breath, like I do
and I wonder how the song sounds
when they sing it loud.
Outside the city where the gulls wheel
the stench of what was left
rises like the breath of the smiling men -
eyes narrow - faces creased
gap-teeth ready.
Their felted suits are soiled,
but it seems only I can see.
Swans flee in formation and a dog barks.
Perhaps the dog is singing too.
I rest on the bridge and notice lights in windows.
Some click on and off like lighthouse beams.
The wind licks my face
as green amber red smears to sunset.

Scrapman

He was born out of the landscape
his brow a ploughed field,
first cry the call of a crow,
first breath drawing clouds across the sky
to empty iron-rich rain onto the hillside
flooding the streets,
drenching his skin,
seeping into his blood,
filling his heart,
confusing his thoughts
and sealing his fate.
Now he sweeps leaves into piles
and with the leaves himself,
and the stories of when he was young.
His bones crack like sticks on a bonfire,
the only sound in the stillness of the yard
where abandoned machines sit like giant crab shells.
A trail of smoke lifts above bare trees,
stark shards against a blurred sky,
as striking as his thoughts.
Unspoken words that used to have meaning
hang in the air like breath
from lips that remember how to kiss
but don't chose to any more.

Hayley Green

A Closer Look

I presented to them, the three heads: two women and a man. I sat in the office as they tumbled out their scripted monologues. They asked me to show them. As I rolled up my sleeves and unbuttoned my trousers their heads morphed into magnifying glasses. Their tongues rolled from their rimmed lips, snaked along the floor and from the back of their throats marched the needles. They sewed my face first – my ears, my lips and then they sewed my hands to the chair. The heads said it wasn't so bad, opened their report books and made notes as they stitched me up. Next came the brushes, two by two, they moved along my arms and legs, sweeping away any visible signs of damage, then retreated, rolling their tongues back into their mouths. They asked me to wait whilst they wrote their reports. So I did. As they scribbled, peering over me, their magnifying glasses caught the rays of the sun and I burned into dust and the brushes marched out once again, sweeping me under the carpet. The reports read *the job is done*.

Seeing

My sister's fingernails are etching themselves into
my skin. She wants me to feel her eye on me. As
she digs further I curl my toes as tightly as they
will go in my boots until the skin in the creases
pinches together. My mind flicks between the pain
she pushes into my palms and back to my toes – a
transference of pelting pins spreading up and down
my body.

If I focus on my toes it lessens the desire to look at
her, my sister, that great eye. The more I think about
it, the tighter her grip becomes, as if she is letting
me know she can see my thoughts – Back to my
toes – I wonder what else she knows. I wonder if I
squeeze my toes tighter she will stop being able to
see me.

I can feel it in my pocket – Back to my toes –
Maybe she knows I took it – Her grip becomes
tighter –Maybe she can see it with her great eye.
Don't look at it – Back to my toes.

I try to keep my hand still, try not to plunge it into my
pocket. Her grip tightens. I miss the feel of silk between
my fingers – Back to my toes – she looked for it this
morning. Her eye is angry. Her nails dig deeper.

Mother said she'd buy her a new one but she knows I took it. I can feel her eye seeing my lie as I tie the ribbon around my fingers – Back to my toes. I scrunch them a little closer together. Just for a second I feel my sister's grip loosen and then squeeze tighter and tighter. I know she knows. She always knows – Back to my toes.

I play with my ribbon when I get back to my bedroom. I lock the door and close the curtains to be certain her eye can't see. I walk over to my chest in the corner of my room and pull out the toys – footballs, spinning tops – until I get to my secret.

A few days ago Mother had set down the laundry on my bed and left to check on the dinner cooking in the kitchen. I tried to resist taking it but I couldn't help but imagine the feel of the petticoat against my legs.

Now I have the whole outfit I lift the dress from the chest and slide it over my head. I take the ribbon she knows I took and slide it through my fingers. My hair isn't long enough but the red matched the dress so perfectly so I tie it around my neck like a scarf.

I just stand there viewing my creation in the mirror.

I am an 8 year old boy and I have stolen my sister's clothes – and she knows. Even now, standing with myself in this room I feel her eye as it burns through me. Somehow she knows – Back to my toes.

Jim Gibson

February 1995 – The Woodland Siege

I remember that it was a drab day and the rain was hovering. It was one of those rains where it almost looked static and you walked into it and got wet rather than it falling on you. None of my friends were willing to leave their houses so I walked up to the woods alone with my toy shotgun under my shoulder, eating a packet of tangy French Fries. If I lick my lips, I can still feel the burn that those years of salt and vinegar sticks left. And, that day, I could feel the eyes of the other children looking out of their windows, wondering why someone had ventured out in such conditions with a shotgun; what possible monster couldn't wait to be killed on a clear day? And, in my mind, I was a hero. I relished their eyes on me, even if they weren't really there, and by the time I reached the entrance to the woods, my hair was dripping and the metal of my gun was too cold to grab for a long period of time.

It was probably a twenty minute walk to the spot I had in mind, an opening with hills on all sides that the motorbikes used. They wouldn't be out today, no one in their right mind was and from the tops of the mounds you could manoeuvre around to get a good sight of all the targets down below. I knew there'd be a few zombies and probably some ninjas (those were tricky to get with a shotgun) but I didn't know what else would be there on a day like today, it was a case of going to find out. I balanced on the log over the stream that we'd all struggled to place there in the summertime and carefully moved up, up, up, avoiding the dense patches of mud that shoes often got completely lost in.

When I got close to the clearing, I heard voices and frowned. I so badly wanted to be the only person out there, I hadn't even seen a dog walker, but now there were these voices that ruined everything. Why should they be allowed out on a day like this? I went into army mode and scurried around the perimeter of the voices, working my way over. I hid behind a bush and stuck my head through to see what was happening. There was five of them, old hippy types, two women and three men, well they looked old to me back then anyway, and they'd built this structure using four trees that stood in a square. It was a treehouse but a grand thing, way up in the sky with pegs dug into one of the trees to climb up. They had a pulley system set up and the men were hoisting what looked like a small whale into the air while the women fetched buckets of water from the stream and chucked them over it. The men were having trouble pulling it up and as it got higher, one of the women had to climb up the pegs and the other now handed her the buckets to douse it with. The whale occasionally made a noise that seemed far too quiet for its size. I watched this for a while until the whale finally reached the top and the woman somehow managed to swing it inside the treehouse. This is when I noticed the funnel on top to collect the rain water and drip it down over the beast. They were up to no good and I knew it. I went over with my shotgun raised and they looked at me. One of them went to speak and something came over me, before I knew it I popped them off one by one, BANG BANG BANG BANG and a final BANG. Five head-shots, turn and shoot. I was sure that they were criminals. I climbed into the treehouse and looked at the whale. It groaned at me to be put out of its misery so I grabbed a knife that laid with a hammer and some other tools to one side and raised it above my head. I looked away as I stuck it deep inside the blubber and carved it open. When I looked back I saw jewels of all colours spilling out and shining and thought about how all the others would never believe it. How they'd all wish that they were out, today of all days.

I'll never forget that siege; it was marvellous.

Trouble on the Lawn

'When she gets out here, I'm gonna fucking wrap this around her fucking head, the dirty slag!'

★★★

It was only last week when I was sat with Lana, in her bedroom, talking all sorts: make up, school, stuff like that. And then we started talking about how much we fancied certain lads in the village. Giving them all ratings out of ten. I gave Terry Walker a 1 because he's a little tramp and no-one likes him and Lana agreed with me. And we pretty much agreed all the way until she sheepishly gave Connor fucking Goodson a 10! I said 'Are you kidding, he's a 6 at best!' But when she talked about him and she said that she proper fancied him and kept going all red and daft, I saw it was real.

At the youth club, a couple of nights later, we were with everyone and I nudged her when Connor walked in with his mates. He was the biggest with one of them curly tops on his head. He was sort of the leader of them lot. Lana looked at me and quietly told me not to say anything; it'd turned out that Chantelle had been going out with him. Chantelle was small and skinny with long blonde hair but not attractive at all. She was hard, too. She was one of them that, when you hang out at the train station, she'd gob off and start on as many people as she could when they got off the trains, 'What you looking at, ya cunt!' and all that.

They didn't look too much like they were together at the youth club, though. Some of them there would just sit on the settee near enough shagging all night but I don't think I even saw them talk to each other that night. It was when me and Lana were outside having a fag that we decided it was more of Chantelle's bullshit, that she'd made it up and that, if you asked Connor about it, then he'd probably be fuming. Probably go over to her and tell her to not spread shit about him. Lana's more shy than me, though, so she wouldn't go and ask him about it. When we were back inside, I saw him looking at his phone, leant on a wall, a bit away from his mates who were sat behind him on the PS3. I went over when Chantelle and everyone had gone round the corner to sit in a room at the side. He laughed when I asked him, I knew he would. He said, 'Well sorta, but not really,' like, he said they'd been texting and that but they hadn't actually done anything yet. I asked him what he thought of Lana and he shrugged but anyone with eyes can see that Lana is FAR better looking than Chantelle and not half as scruffy, either.

The next night, me and Lana were out, just walking round the village, when we got a text from one of the other girls saying that someone had set fire to the old nursing home so we went down and sat on the wall with all of them to watch it burn. It was hot and felt odd to see a building that had been boarded up all of my life now glowing and alive. Flames spat out of the roof and windows. Everyone felt the energy. People said that Chantelle and her brother had started it and that's why they were nowhere to be seen. I was mainly on my own, laughing with the lads as they threw loads of stuff up onto the flames. Lana and Connor were still sat on the wall behind me, I could hear her laugh every now and then and they *did* look good together. The next thing I remember was the fire engine's lights and everyone scattering, one way or another.

On Saturday night, she messaged me to say that she needed me to come round QUICK. I asked her what was up and she just said to come round, told me to bring my school stuff and stop over. Her dad worked nights so I stayed over hers quite a lot. I walked around in my PJs and dressing gown with my school bag and a plastic bag of clothes and, when I got there, she showed me this text from Connor: *Wat u up 2? Bin finkin bout u all day xxx.* 'What do I say back?' she asked me. 'Oh my god!

Just telling him you're chillin and stuff.' All night the texts came back and forth and we talked through the best answer each time. To sound into him but not desperate. They started getting kinky later on in the night and it was getting harder to know what to put back so we told him we'd gotta go and just left him there. Wanting more. When we were in Lana's bed, she asked me if I'd ever sent any messages like that to anyone, you know, like dirty talk and all that. I was facing the back of her head but I could tell she was wide awake and I could hear her fiddling with the carpet. I told her I sort of had and that it wasn't that bad, that it was to Jamie Spearman and that he was so into me while we were doing it. I tell her how I even sent him a few pics to show him that I'm not frigid and that he said that I was beautiful.

The next day, I got took home from school because my nan had died. All of the family were round and when Lana text that night to ask me to come round, I told her that I couldn't and told her just to carry on from last night. I was dying to see what she was saying to him so I asked her to text me what she put each time but she wouldn't. It was such a downer at home. Nan had been in a home in the next town since I was about 8 and no one really went to see her anymore, anyway.

The next day at school it was like I could feel the rumours going round as soon as I walked in the gate, there was just that feeling in the air that something was happening on the hush hush. I didn't know what it was but I could feel it going round everyone. I was looking for Lana to get the juicy goss and see what she actually text last night, when the bell went and I was sent to tutor. I sat down with my bag on the table in front of me, Mr Grayson wasn't there yet and this pale, ginger kid called Billy came over and sorta laughed and said, 'Your mates in BIG trouble.' I said, 'What you on about, Billy? Ya scrawny little copper dick. How the fuck do you know about anything?' He sat down next to me, 'Shit, you really haven't heard have you?' 'What the fuck you chatting on about?' He leant on the table. 'Well, apparently, Lana was texting Connor.' 'Yeah, and?' 'Well he's going with Crazy Chantelle, that mad head who got kicked out last year.' 'Yeah, I fucking know who Chantelle is, Billy, ya fucking dipshit.' 'Well, Lana was sending nudes last night but it turns out it wasn't Connor. Chantelle had been pretending to be him and now she's gonna PROPER batter Lana.' 'Oh shit, SHIT, SHIT!' I got up to go and find her but Mr Grayson walked in and told me to sit down. I told him it was urgent and said, 'Sir, you don't understand, I've GOT to find Lana; it's an emergency.' but he told me to sit down again and I couldn't get out of it.

It wasn't until break that I saw her and sat down with her. She started crying as soon as we got to the back of the tennis courts and showed me the messages she'd been getting from Chantelle and everyone else: SLAG, SLUT, SKET, SCRUFFY CUNT, they were non-stop. Chantelle's messages were the worst though, she was saying that she was going to smash her face in with a brick and things like that. I looked up and saw Connor and the other lads walking past a bit further down, laughing. They shouted with their hand circling their mouths, across the tennis court, 'SLAG' in one big chorus. She looked up at me with a face full of snot and said, 'He said he liked me at the fire, what the fuck's happening?' I said to her, 'Let's just make it through school and then worry about it later, yeah?' but she said she couldn't stay and we ended up sneaking out the back way, over the farmer's field.

On the bus home, we were both quiet. There were some year sevens behind us who were bunking off and we could hear them sniggering to each other. Even though we didn't say anything, I knew we were both expecting her to be at the bus stop when we got off. I don't know why she would be there but she was everywhere in our heads. As it pulled into the village there was Wendy who worked in the Welfare and the old man, Whistler: no Chantelle. We walked that fast back to Lana's that we might as well have been running. Her dad was in so we snuck up the jitty and hid out in the playhouse that we hadn't been in for years. When we heard him leave a few hours later we slipped back out and went into the empty house. She sat down at the table with her head in her hands. She didn't know what to do so I told her to give me her phone and we text Chantelle saying that Lana was sorry and all that but all we got back was: 2 l8 u w8.

And this is where we are now. It's got dark and they're all outside. About 10 of them. Chantelle's shouting 'GET OUT HERE NOW, I'M GONNA KICK YER FUCKING HEAD IN, YA SLUT.' And the lads shout, too. They bang on the door. I peek outside from the upstairs window in the darkness and see them standing there with tennis rackets and a block of wood. Connor storms over, saying something about booting the door down and he goes for it. Kicking as hard as he can, rattling the whole house while the girls all shout about Lana. I can see other houses peeking out of their windows, their faces lit by mobile phones, but no one *does* anything. There's more shouting and Lana is shaking. Crying. She tries to shout that she'll 'Fucking stab em all' but it comes out broken and not loud. I'm ready to hold her back but she doesn't move. Then I hear, 'DO IT, CONNOR.' and there's a smash downstairs. The living room. There's more screams but they fade. I go downstairs and see the handle of a tennis racket through the glass of the window. It looks like that's it for now. I go back upstairs and put my arms around Lana and can't help but think that I'm probably going to be in for it too if they saw I was here.

Panya Banjoko

Insomniac's Count

moles with sunglasses,
the spots of a hundred ladybirds,
the flapping wings of a starling murmuration,
a platoon of poets that shout
speak the truth! speak the truth!
the smell of a mystical dragon's breath,
the moan of mothers who are bereft,
the notes of a lonely soldier's bugle,
the 'v' shaped trail of a water vole,
twigs that make up a thousand nests,
the step of each child lost without hope,
the length of a giraffes neck, multiply it by a yard
and divide it by a quarter of a metre,
the teeth of a crocodile as it slinks in water,
Dalmatians' spots,
a hippograph's oath,
the tiny tremors in a heart,
the cracks in a life,
the nerve endings,
gas encased in chambers,
the hunger,
the fraud,
hands that choke,
count this and all this and this and this and more
if sleep remains amiss
count

beetles with bendy legs,

the hairs on a chimpanzees shoulder,

the number of hands that seek to be picked,

shadows that lurk during the night,

babies born to those who regret and mourn,

the odour of a new day as it dawns,

children who grow up for less and see more,

the squadron of victims made in this place,

the chimes of a hung dead bell,

the rivers we plan to cross,

the shame of tests that rank and order,

the brutes who squash,

the lies told by politicians, subtracted by the people
they deceive and those who believe,

the lips full of the froth of decadence,

clocks ticking,

the locks that imprison,

the clink of keys that flaunt,

the time that is up,

the time that is lost,

the time that is never found,

the wounded,

the fragile,

eyes that beg to be blind,

count this and all this and this and this and more

if sleep remains amiss

count...

Sophie Pickford

Diane Llewella Wolf

LOVE LETTERS

Dear Mr Cameron,

I have been to a meeting today in which a report on how austerity measures have impacted the people of Nottingham in the last 4.5 years was discussed. The same measures that you seemed so shocked about the repercussions of in your own (very wealthy) constituency. As you may be aware, should be aware, Nottingham is the 17th most deprived constituency in the UK... I would imagine Witney is somewhere near the most affluent. Are you equally as shocked and appalled by the impacts of your measures here in Nottingham? How aware are you even of the impacts of your measures here or in other not so affluent areas?

I am not a politician. I have no credentials and perhaps have no right to comment or tell you how to do your job but much as I get that as a society there needs to be more personal responsibility and more living within the means of the budget available... I don't get why you think it's acceptable for the most vulnerable and least culpable members of society to suffer the most...Disabled adults and children. Children from poor families. Adults on low wages. Single parent families, especially those on low wages. Refugees. Why are you forcing councils and local authorities to cut back on essential services that help to keep us, as a community safe and healthy and happy...? Why is it not the upper echelon of society that are paying more into the pot? Oh, is it maybe because you are from that section of society and you have more sympathy for 'your own' and the desire to maintain their privileged status quo, even if it is at the expense of others. I mean, I just can't quite comprehend how bankers have been allowed to get away with all that they have for so long, why certain businesses get away without having to pay tax, Why it is that the queen has had a 7% pay rise (does she really need an extra £2 million a year?) and yet so many working people are expected to subsist on less than the living wage... not Mr Osbourne's ideas on the living wage, I mean The living wage, as worked out and agreed upon by Living Wage Foundation.. Why is it that public sector worker's pay has been frozen for 4 years (with another 4due) when MP's have been given a 10% rise? Are you more worthy? Is your job more integral and important? Why is it that social mobility is being thwarted from every angle? We have the highest university fees here in the UK compared to

Western Europe... And seeing as education is one of the best ways to scale the social and economic ladder, surely that should be priority if you actually want everyone to prosper? In Nottingham we have one of the highest rates of unemployment in the UK coupled with one of the lowest rates of pay. Roughly £5K less a year for average salary than everywhere else outside of London. How is pushing the most vulnerable people in society deeper into poverty the answer? Unless it is as simple as you just don't believe in equality, fairness and diversity... unless you believe that the people who live in and come from positions of privilege somehow deserve that status and in reflection those who are currently marginalised in society, those made vulnerable by virtue of circumstance, heritage, class, gender, being born into poverty, disability, having the temerity to be seeking refuge from fleeing horrors that you or I cannot fully comprehend, that these people also deserve this and don't deserve to be supported in engaging in that carrot on a string fallacy of 'social mobility'.

It seems you have no qualms about dropping bombs that could (I know you have weakly tried to disagree with this) and will kill innocent civilians-babies, children, mothers, fathers, brothers, sisters... All strangers and statistics to you I'm sure... So it should come as no surprise that you have no qualms about destroying the fabric of our society here by increasing the gap between rich and poor to the point where huge swathes of children, families, PEOPLE will be left destitute and hopeless... All the while you and your kind will be growing fat off the backs of their, our demise... In fact, why don't you use one (poverty and destitution) to fund the other (war)? Oh, you already have...no, not just you... All of the MP's that voted for the air strikes AND all of the people who voted for you...

You seem to suggest that you are trying to protect us as a society... By perpetuating the cycle of violence with IS and in turn helping to engender radicalisation and hatred on all sides AND funding that perpetuation, that show of power and dominance by using money you say we just don't have to make the UK a fairer more equal place for ALL. You say you want to create peace and yet you drop bombs on areas THAT WILL have civilians present. You say we have to all take responsibility, but are you prepared to take responsibility when the proverbial shit hits the fan – which it undoubtedly will... Are you willing to take responsibility for the impending crisis here in Britain? Pushing so many families and groups of people into poverty and at the same time eradicating the services that provide security and assistance to those in need. Where do you think that will end? Can you really in your heart of hearts justify any of this to yourself?

£508K per air strike is what I heard... How many air strikes till you've won David? Really...add it up, both literally and morally...

Diane

Dear Eric Clapton,

I write this as an open letter to you in reference to
your apology for 'semi-racist' comments in the 70's.

I was born in 1976, the year that you made your
speech about how good white British folk should
vote for Enoch Powell cos you didn't want Britain
to become a 'black colony' and how you wanted the
'coons' and 'wogs' to go back to their own countries.

I was born to two immigrant parents, one from the
West Indies another from India. I grew up in an
environment that was not only racially tense but also
dangerous. Cos people like you, who held positions
of power - a power that came from your birth right
of being white more than your talent - used that
power to disseminate racist ideologies...

No, Powell and you and all the others who believed
that Britain should remain white and that People of
Colour were somehow
Lesser than you and a stain on your social fabric did

not get your way, but the legacy that you have all left is something we still see around us today and in fact has had a massive resurgence of late.

YOU and many other white musicians used black musicians and black music to build an empire. You literally stole that music, put a white stamp on it and made yourself rich and powerful. I don't care that you fetishised a black woman and called her your girlfriend. I don't care that there were black people in your social circle you called friends.

I don't care that you were drunk, off your face and that it was 40 odd years ago. Saying the word 'sorry' does not quite cut it.

Here is what I, as a woman of colour who has had to endure not only out and out racism throughout her life but also the gentle, slow, drip drip effect of othering that comes from the 'us and them' rhetoric that what you and others like you have said, here is what I think is fitting for a man in your privileged position – if sorry is anything more than a cheap PR trick from an old man who has had his cake now and can spare some crumbs – to do.

In the name of transparency release the video footage of that speech from 1976... if you are unclear what speech I am referring to, it is the one in which you state this;

"I don't want you here, in the room or in my country," Clapton declared. "Listen to me, man! I think we should vote for Enoch Powell. Enoch's our man. I think Enoch's right, I think we should send them all back. Stop Britain from becoming a black colony. Get the foreigners out.

Get the wogs out. Get the coons out. Keep Britain white. I used to be into dope, now I'm into racism. It's much heavier, man.

Fucking wogs, man. Fucking Saudis taking over London. Bastard wogs. Britain is becoming overcrowded and Enoch will stop it and send them all back. The black wogs and coons and Arabs and fucking Jamaicans and fucking… don't belong here, we don't want them here.

This is England, this is a white country, we don't want any black wogs and coons living here. We need to make clear to them they are not welcome. England is for white people, man. We are a white country. I don't want fucking wogs living next to me with their standards. This is Great Britain, a white country. What is happening to us, for fuck's sake?"

Using your sizable wealth and power, actually DO

something to make amends... fund organisations that aim to promote black creatives or fight for the rights of people of colour in the UK like BLMUK.

Make yourself seen and heard as an advocate for BME issues. Speak out and urge others in your position to do the same.

Read up on ideas around white privilege and structural racism and be open about how YOU have benefitted from these things.

One last and perhaps insignificant point but I loved your song Layla as a teenager... it was almost my song of choice to lose my virginity to. You were a talented man in your own way but I hope you understand that the platform you were given was based upon doors being closed to others by virtue of their ethnicity and sometimes gender.

That makes it doubly abhorrent that you have been part of the fabric of racism in my country. I hope you are suitably ashamed.

Thank you for your time

Diane

Dear Piers Morgan,

Even before you open your mouth to allow
words to spill like lava from a dysentery ridden
arsehole, like the blood of the innocent, like cum
from a prostitutes mouth, I see a human being
riding high on the back of so many positions of
privilege... the smugness basically of a white, middle
to upper classed, educated man... I see it and I'm
arrested momentarily, lulled perhaps into a false
sense (bought on by the cacophonic messages all
around me, us, each and every one of us, about
the importance and rightness and perfectness of
someone occupying those identities) of security
that you are an intelligent, well thought out and
reasoned individual.

But then you speak... or write (in this particular
case) and I'm reminded that there is nothing quite
as remarkable as the confidence of a white mediocre
man.

You suffer from the kind of poverty I find slightly

painful to witness, hear, be reminded exists - yes - it brings out the snob in me - cos you seem to exist in a bubble of delusion, short sightedness and self-absorption. You are, what I would truly describe as an oxygen thief... you and many others like you who are so wrapped up in self-importance that you have lost one of the most beautiful things it is to be human...; empathy....

"Let boys be damn boys. Let men be damn men"

On the one hand, that comment could be reduced to the snivelling of a child who has realised that he cannot have his own way all the time... a little tanty by an overly milk fed boy. On the other it is a dangerous assertion for someone in your position to make. A dangerous comment and response to an advert trying to address the issue, proven fucking issue we have in this society with toxic masculinity. Yes, let's just let boys be boys and men be the men this society teaches them to be cos it's working out just great isn't it? Never mind what someone's ethnicity is when they've engaged in violence or what the gender is of their victim. Let's look at the proportion of perpetrators that are men. Let's look at the statistics of rape, domestic violence... let's look at the perpetrators of that... let's look at the #metoo campaign... let's listen and see if we can hear the voices of the millions of women, worldwide who have died, been abused, shafted financially, politically, spiritually, at the hands of men. Oh wait... you can't hear most of them cos they are still living under the prevailing attitude (prevailing because it is endemic) that boys will just be boys. They are those silently oppressed.

Men like you make me feel unsafe in this world. People like you who could use your intelligence to fully understand this epidemic... understand the history of it, the hows and whys and use that to form an opinion that was well balanced and thought out. Use your privileges and position to attempt to make some changes in the world... and not simply for the women in your lives... but because you had a fully operative moral compass. But, alas...you do not... and I go back to my initial snobbery... you, Mr Morgan are poor... you suffer from a poverty of the soul that is utterly abhorrent. And inexcusable.

Signed – a woman who has spent a life time feeling the hand of toxic masculinity upon her face, up her skirt, round her throat...

Keith Ford

'And for that Reason, I'm Out'

Because a television left on standby offers far kinder opportunities for reflection than a friend left on standby.

Because someone, somewhere with Sambuca-singed soul is wiping tears from their Street Pastor flip-flops.

Because it's Saturday Night and once again I put my faith and hopes and dreams into the autopilot, autographing hands of men-children who happen to be wearing the right coloured stripes.

Because it's Sunday night and that is actually reason to attend, rather than not attend, the gig of choice.

Because I have no savings and it seems a little late in the day to start worrying about that now.

Because it is literally a little late in the day and I can park for free.

Because my 40s are nearly my 50s and I can speak for free.

Because this is England and I can talk for…. England.

Because the relevance of age
is the only elephant uncaged
around here.

Because the smooth arse
of cougars
can sometimes simply be down to the right kind of

control.

Because I remain an optimist who no longer needs
to be pissed.

Because I still have my looks depending on who is
doing the looking.

Because I still have my hair depending on who's
doing the cutting.

Because I've had a shit day.

Because I've had a great day.

Because we were put on this planet to socialise

and make eyes

and admire thighs

and spot lies

and disguise

and then prise

Screwed-up victory from the jaws of defeat,

Chewed-up heads from the jaws of lions,

Clued-up romance from the jaws of the Tyne.

And for that reason I'm out.

A Cloudless Night in London

The message from Facebook read
"Good afternoon Keith, the clouds will be clearing
tonight in London…."

The words seem to massage my tightened neck
muscles,
gently rotating thumbs, kneading me,
nearly as much as I was needing them.

The clouds will be clearing tonight in London
and me and my lass will dance again to songs from
our youth
and new songs we have yet to be introduced to
friends of friends
with little in common
except a love uncommon.

Times of lives and rock of ages,
where age is irrelevant,
I'm younger than the DJ
That's all that I need to know.

I know these songs the young uns don't recognise
and I recognise what the young uns are going
through.
Groups of them stand and chat on the dance floor,

eating into valuable dance space
like vampires,
or umpires
with somebody else's jumpers tied round their
waists,
somebody else's jumpers, somebody else's good
times.

I have no answers
for the non-dancers
but a little word of advice....

Stop trying
to look like you're
not trying.

Leanne Moden

Canalside

The neon at the bar is blazing blue –
I never could resist a Friday night.
The old boys in the back are spinning songs,
while I taste cigarette ash on my tongue.
I'm drinking, so I barely feel the cold;
reality is blurred around its edge.

Outside, I am a blade. I take my edge
and slice the water open, till the blue
comes flowing out to wash away the cold.
I never could resist a Friday night,
the taste of revolution on my tongue.
I've let this city sing her marching songs,

and fill my mind with myths and lies. The songs
that set my long-held principles on edge.
The gin explodes like starlight on my tongue,
behind my eyes the bubbles bursting blue.
I never could resist a Friday night.
Sometimes I want to plunge into the cold

and taste the water on my lips. This cold
reminds me of the litany of songs
I've hurled into the bleak November night.
I make my home beside the water's edge
and cradled cans in fingers tinged with blue.

Some said that I had cut away my tongue

or worn it down to silence. No, my tongue
now only speaks to those who feel the cold.
A sharpened shifting shard of silver blue,
that ties my mind with misremembered songs.
Invisible, I skim the city's edge,
and beg for change while you ignore the night.

I never could resist a Friday night;
inertia's blade serrated on my tongue.
Reality is glassy at its edge
like water in the lock, so hard and cold.
I've wrapped myself in all the city's songs,
like bruises on my chest in black and blue.

The cold is creeping round perception's edge
so, drink and sing and gaze beyond the blue
with night still fizzing on my freezing tongue.

Sitting on a bench at the City Arboretum, Nottingham

After James Wright

Over my head, I see the humbug-striped magpie
Standing on the thick black branch,
Shaking cherry blossom to the ground like confetti.
Down the hill, behind the empty bandstand,
The laughter of a hundred ducks
Merges with the swoop of passing tram carriages.
To my right,
In a field of spilled-paint grass, flung with buttercups,
A bright blue crisp packet
Glitters like an unearthed hoard.
I lean back, as the evening light lingers in the trees.
A woman walks past, pushing an empty pram.
Life without suffering is meaningless.

Trevor Wright

Reap as you Sow

A Sidewinder skittering across the desert floor
clackkkk of a security card opening up the door
hummm of the cold box at sixty eight degrees
hissssss of a bank of high definition screens.

It's a buzzzzz of real time intel firmly under control
the zoooooom of the feed live from today's patrol
a suuuuuck of the teeth and a sharp intake of breathe
as the pilot he targets a credible imminent threat.

The authorised man in the loop he slowly takes stock
of the cross hair on the screen now firmly locked
on the truck as it sputttters its way across the sands
then the click of the joystick at the pilots command.

A puuurrrr of low cost option engineered stealth
kaachiiink of the catch as the loaded deck is dealt
swoooosh on release of the sanction on the rail
the whuuumpf of objectives taken out on the trail.

There's no skin in the game of targeted strikes
nor risk from devices planted every few mikes
just the scribble of a pen signing rules of engagement
and the drone from above inflicting mental torment

with the spooks on the hill well protected from the
    sound
of wailing grieving families seeing body parts on
    the ground
and the silence of the world each time more debt is
    fastened
round children's necks by remote and frosty
    fingered assassins.

In Such Times

In such times,
unless we are heedful,
blood red clouds
will ricket our children
lacerate skin, pockmark hearts
strip dreams back to bleached bones
entombed under squalid mounds of rust

We have been better than this
and can be again.
If we learn to distil today's rain
into tomorrow's spirit,
to write ourselves,
to write ourselves greater stories,
than the stories that are burying us today.

Michelle 'The Mother' Hubbard

Dad Doesn't Deserve Dementia

This week
10 cups of tea a day
have been washed away
with mouthfuls of messy medication.
He's sick of the staff nurse
wagging her tale
and barking out foreign instructions.

They serve him mountains of manky mash potato,
but when it comes around
he's just a mash potato hater.
And he curses
the nurse that's
been posing as a waiter.

This week
he struggles to swallow any information,
whilst I sit choking on the truth.
He lies in a bed he didn't make,
reading the daily prescription,
but his eyes are not open.

This week
(Or was it last)
I hated the fact
that disposable nappies are not just for babies,

and there will never be any potty training.

This week
Dad tells me
that the young Greek
male nurse, is his daddy.
So I smile and say
"Hello,   Granddad,   I'm   Michelle,   your
granddaughter."

And I wonder –

Is this just some weird 'time shift'
like Back To The Future?
Maybe this isn't dementia?
Maybe my dad is a *time traveller*?
Maybe 'shit-bollocks-arse-cock'
is some secret code I'm supposed to unlock,
or remembered? …
… Instead of feeling embarrassment and anger.

This week
as I spoon him mouth-loads
of manky mash potato
I want to scream out
"Stop it now! This game has gone on
for far too long!

I've learned my lesson!"

This week
when I demand he drinks and eats,
saying "If not, you'll get sick and weak!"
And he spits an eyeful at me,
I want to cry out "Daddy,
pick me up and rescue me!"
But dad cries out before me
"Oh, please, Michelle, stop it! Please stop it!"

And I wished I could.
I wished to God I could stop it:
Stop this runaway nightmare.
Find him a care home that genuinely cares.
Take him by the hand
and travel back to a time-band
when Alzheimer's and Dementia
weren't part of our family picture.

This week,
or was it last?
Or is it next week?   … I'm lost!?

Miggy Angel

Tenderness

He watched through a crack
in the door-jamb. Saw the man
sat upon the bath hem. Watched

how he unspooled the fingers
of his hand. Ligament octopus,
ligatures unfurled and clasped

the silver scalpel handle. He
could have entered the bathroom
then. Instead, transfixed, he watched

the man cut each wrist with an identical
movement. Right, then left. He had
never seen such tenderness.

The Return

The boy leaves prison a man.
Returns to the scene of the crime. Or,
the gentrification, or what's left

of his home. The locale of his cradle
is unrecognisable. No neighbours
remain in the neighbourhood. Same

concrete under foot, same cloud
overhead. All the old abodes are razed,
the new-builds house no-one he knows.

He's back on the street of his birth,
knocks upon a door. At random. Awaits
the middle-class incumbents. Fingers

the silver blade held in the pocket
of his battered leather smother. Hears
his mother call his name.

The Knife Drawer

Existential dread always sounded so
gentle. The genteel classes

privileged to be afflicted
with a literary genre. Poorfolk

never had the option of Existentialism
just got sectioned instead.

Boy-body filled like a tank
with the lead of a burning terror tell me

where do you hide the knives
in your existential poems?

Gemma Fenyn

Suicide off Farmfoods' Rooftop

Did it jump or was it pushed?
A pigeon landed at my foot.
With a thud.
Wings fanned out as it scraped,
To regain a semblance of what it was.
But too late.
I watched and I knew.
Before the bile trickled from its beak,
Before its beady brow reflected panic,
What came next.

I couldn't break its neck,
I didn't have the strength,
And yet,
I couldn't allow it to slowly die.
Outside Farmfoods.
On a Tuesday night.
I just couldn't let it die.

I wonder if I'm completely mad sometimes,
If there's something inside of me,
That's not quite right…

I carefully scoop the limp bird up.
Everything's going to be fine.

You never buy me flowers,
And, you've never been a fan
Of overblown gestures.
When you refuse to conform
To this fallacy,
Well, it brings out an ugly
Side of me.

Would it really hurt?
To buy me one bunch of flowers?
You never bring me flowers.

But here I skulk in,
Like a shamefaced cat,
And present you with
A docile
Dying
Bird.

Whose insides, now liquified,
Are gradually exiting,
Pooling in the palm of my hand,
Trickling down my skin,

Into a pool on the Lino.

And then there is a lapse in time.
Where your eyes meet mine.

And for a few seconds,
We have a blazing row.
In complete silence.

You break first 'Has it…'
'Yes it's shit in the car.'
'But…' and here I falter,
'It's dying…and I couldn't…I just couldn't…'

I am your mission.
You choose to accept me.

We place the pigeon
In a carrier bag. sombrely.

With your office boy hands,
You feel its neck. Crack.

We commit it
to the wheelie bin.
And I begin to relax.

Sometimes I can be everything.
All too often I am nothing.
The only thing I have to give
In this life is my art.
The only thing I have of any worth
Is my verse.

But for you.
When it comes to you.

I have no words.

The Pioneer

Back in the day,
When everything was gay.
School was gay.
Maths was gay.
Cricket was definitely gay.
But no, not you mate,
One hundred and ten percent straight,
As I watched you sashay,
All the way from P.E to D.T,
To heckles and jeers,
Of shit stabber, fag and batty boy.
And you'd just look at us,
Whisper 'it's fine'.
But there were things unsaid
Behind your eyes.
Too much said
In my silence.
Things best left,
Behind the bike shed,
Where you casually inhaled on a cigarette
And we kissed for the very first time...
I say kissed,
It was more a soggy, uncoordinated compressing of
lips,
Before you threw your head back,
In a giggling fit.

I would have been your lavender wife.
A quick fix for your fracturing mind.
It's just an incidental lie…

But you were braver than I could ever be,
When they ripped you out of the closet.

I'm sorry.

I last saw you on Pelham Street.
You were all, Stephen Gately curtains,
Platforms, piercings and pvc pants,
Crop top and that smile.
You were out and proud and
really fucking loud…

So what happened?
Did you love too much?
Did you trust too hard?
Did he lead you on
And break your heart?
Or did you just get really fucking tired?
Of every school day being a constant fight?
Of the shame that stalked you
Into your adult life?

The grapevine muttered suicide.

And the rest was silence.

Anthem For a Doomed Statistic

They say that you are broken. You are anything but
    that.
Though, sometimes, your ribbon veins unravel,
Searching for some oblivion and your gut knots,
With the promise of the abyss.
Broken, you are not.

It was on one incidental day,
When the world, for the most part, seemed
    unchanged,
That you gazed upon the scattered shards of your
    life,
And remembered all that had been.

A handprint immortalised on a sliver of window
    pane,
Kept her with you for days.
There you danced beyond the looking glass,
    collecting
Each fragment on the way. Resting your memories
    in a
New place.

When the sun rose again, you knew that you had
    been
Forever changed.

They say that we are broken. But we are not.
Sure our backs are bent with the weight of our
    shame,
And on each of our tables, there's an empty space,
But have you seen what we've done with this
    mosaic?

These tiles reflect pain and heartbreak, the journey
    of
A coward who grew to be brave, a murmur that
    thrived
In the darkest place, these inconsequential pieces,
dragged back from the fringes, scream more
Than those great institutions ever could say.

We are anchored right here. Breathing.
Taking it day by day.
Wild horses couldn't drag us away.

Ben Williams

An Interesting Story

The café owner, he was called Dio, and he was always saying that he loved the English. He said it so often to Rick and me that we started to wonder why he'd set up his café there in Heranoss, the Dutch and German part of the island, when the English area of Malia was only a short drive down the road. Every morning we would go to the café for breakfast and Dio would hurry out from behind the bar in his white apron, smeared with yellow streaks of egg yolk, and pull a seat out for us both. He was a small, leather skinned man with a horseshoe of hair around his brown-egg head. His bushy eyebrows moved like waves. He was always laughing.

'Heavy night?' he would say. 'Always party people you English! I love it!'

At that time, Rick and I were camping at a site about ten minutes down the coast from Dio's place. The plan, originally, had been to go island hopping. Stay a night there, a day here, that sort of thing. But the plan had only lasted until we arrived at our first stop in Heranoss, when we saw the beautiful women there. Women so beautiful, I knew I wanted to spend the entire summer there. They were so beautiful that, given the option of an endless uneventful summer, I would have stayed there until the day the sun burnt out. We'd never seen women like this before, all tanned and tall with pushed up hair. Even the campsite owner's daughter was a stunner. It was amazing. We were eighteen and from a very small town in a very grey part of England. It was our first time abroad.

Every evening we would dress up as best we could and share a little pot of hair gel we had bought from a corner shop. When we were all ready, our hair spiked up or slicked down, we'd go into town to try and pull, hoping that the beautiful women we found there would be as impressed by our foreignness as we were by theirs. And every night we would fail. And then we would drink some more. And try again. And drink some more, until the sky threatened us with the morning, when we would stagger back to our tents, just ahead of the rising sun, thoroughly drunk, horny and frustrated.

Our morning trips to Dio's café for breakfast were a kind of consolation. The breakfast wasn't bad and he was always happy to see us back, all sweaty and hungover and gasping. He even loved the fact we'd order a pint with our breakfast. He would laugh, loud, and start shouting about how much he loved the English again. The whole café would turn to us and watch Dio slapping our backs and clowning around.

'You crazy guys,' he would call us, as if he had never seen anything so mad as a pint with breakfast.

'You crazy guys, you English.'

'I'm sick of this,' said Rick, once Dio had left to serve another table of customers. He had been quiet all morning. He looked at his pint on the table with disgust. 'I didn't come here just for this.'

'We'll get lucky,' I told Rick. I thought I knew what he was annoyed about. Last night, we had come very close to pulling two Dutch girls. A little squat, a little plain, but they were far from ugly. As the night had gone on though, we had either got too drunk, or something had happened, and suddenly we had nothing to say to them. Within an hour they'd gone to the toilet and then ditched us.

Rick shook his head at me.

'Don't stress,' I told him. 'We've got a fortnight left here pal.'

'You don't get it man,' said Rick. 'I didn't come all this way to get pissed every night and eat in the same fucking café.'

He looked around him to see if Dio might have heard. Luckily Dio was in the back.

'I came to travel,' he said.

'And what's this then?'

'This? We haven't been any fucking place. I'm going travelling.'

'When?'

'Today,' he said loudly. 'I'm sick of this fucking place.'

We sat for a moment in silence and Rick began to drink his pint. When he had finished he shouted Dio over. I thought he was going to ask for the bill, but instead he ordered another pint. I realised he was getting drunk in case he had to travel alone. Rick was a very confident drunk.

'This is the last time you'll see me, pal,' Rick said to Dio when he came over with his pint.

'Ah! Time to go back to England my friends?'

Rick smiled and shook his head. 'I'm going travelling,' he boasted. 'Further down the coast. And then on to a different island.'

'That is good, yes,' said Dio nodding his head. 'Where you go next?'

Rick shrugged.

'Ahhh. You crazy guys eh? You go with wind,' he began to laugh, then stopping very suddenly, he put his hand to his chin so that it was very obvious he was thinking. 'I have idea. One moment.'

Dio hurried behind his bar and came back to our table cradling a small brown bottle and three shot glasses. A new set of customers walked into the café. Dio ignored them and popped the cork off from the bottle and poured out three drinks.

'You guys tried Raki before?'

We hadn't. Dio seemed to love this fact, almost as much as the pints we ordered for breakfast.

'You English guys. You all pints, chips and sausage.'

He poured out three shots. Before we could drink, Dio wanted to do a toast.

'What you do when you travel?' he asked me.

I shrugged. I didn't want to travel, but I knew I would end up going with Rick anyway.

'Same as we do here, probably,' I told Dio. 'Drink and talk to women.'

Dio chuckled. He had become less clown like and more fatherly now that he was about to give a toast.

'Okay. Well, may you have the same fun wherever you go as you had here,' he toasted, and downed his Raki in one.

On the way back to our campsite, Rick and me didn't speak much. The beautiful German and Dutch girls kept passing us by, smiling and talking amongst themselves. They filled the cafes we passed too, smoking at their tables, sipping at their tiny coffees, hundreds of them. I couldn't believe Rick wanted to leave. It made me so mad.

'We've got to stay one more day,' I said to Rick. 'We've got to.'

Rick didn't even look at me. 'You can,' he said.

'What difference will one day make? I asked him. 'None. It makes no difference. Let's stay.'

I was willing to beg if I had to. I wasn't ready to leave. After last night's near miss, I was sure all we needed was one more night. Maybe we just needed to buy them more drinks? Maybe we don't get so drunk? Maybe – just maybe we'd get lucky this time?

But Rick kept on shaking his head.

'These girls aren't like that,' he said to me, an expert all of a sudden. 'You can't just drink with them and expect them to fuck you. They've got a bit of class. You need to get them interested with a good story or something.'

'So we'll try that tonight then. What's your problem?'

Rick tutted. 'What story do you know then? They want to hear about something different. About travel. About the world.'

'Travel?'

'Yeah, about travel. Lots of interesting stories happen when you travel. Not like here. Nothing interesting happens here. It's like everywhere else, but with shit loads of sun. We gotta go someplace interesting. Look,' he stopped talking and turned to me. 'I realised this last night. Pretty foreign girls fuck interesting boys. Fact.'

'So we need to travel first?'

'Exactly.'

I wasn't convinced, but I could see that Rick was already a little drunk and very confident in what he was saying. He spotted a bar that was just opening up and went inside. There were mini maps on the bar, so Rick ordered a couple of pints and we took one of the maps to a table. After a couple more drinks, Rick was happy he had found a good place to go. It involved a long hike to get there and was set someway back from a large beach. It was an area miles from the usual tourist spots.

We had a couple more drinks and walked down the last stretch of the coast towards our campsite. I was starting to feel pretty drunk. The sun was up high and I was hot and tired too. Now that I knew I'd be leaving soon everything around me started to have a slight tint of nostalgia. I had convinced myself that this stretch of cafes and bars and beach was unlike anywhere else in the world. Even if further along the coast we found even more beautiful women, I knew I would miss this place.

'Hey, Rick,' I said to him. I was starting to change my mind about leaving. 'When are we going? It's getting me down, knowing I've got to leave.'

He paused. 'I…' then trailed off.

I realised Rick wasn't listening. We had turned the last corner towards our campsite and now Rick was staring towards it and a crowd of people, maybe eight or nine in total, stood there at the edge of the rocks. We walked over to them. They were chatting in their own language all hushed, yet excited sounding, as if they were panicking. I couldn't understand it.

'What's going on?' I asked Rick.

Rick pointed at the sea, at a floating lilo. So what? Then, twenty yards further out in the distance I saw a man, flapping his arms about. He was too far away for us to hear him shouting. If he was shouting.

'Is he alright?' I said. I knew that he wasn't though. I was just shocked. It seemed so surreal. The sea was remarkably still too, except for the occasional white tipped crease that spread lengthways like a ripple in a pond. A moment passed of utter silence. Then I heard a commotion next to me. Rick was getting undressed. He had already taken off his t-shirt and he was struggling with his jeans. He was too drunk to stand on one leg to lift the other one out. He had to lean against another man there. The crowd now forgot about the man in the sea and turned to Rick, eyes full of expectation.

'Rick,' I said quietly. 'What are you doing?'

Finally, he had managed to take his jeans off and was stood in just his boxers and socks.

'What?' he said.

I put my hand on his shoulder. 'Rick don't fucking do it. You're too drunk.'

He shrugged me off and started to pull at one of his socks.

'Fuck's sake Rick,' I hissed at him under my breath. 'What you doing?'

The crowd turned to look at me. I suppose whether they spoke English or not it was clear that I was telling Rick to stay where he was. I knew that if he ran out there to help that man there was a chance – a good chance, that he'd get into trouble himself. Everyone then would turn to me, to see if I would go and help him, and I knew that I didn't have it in me; I couldn't save that random man, and I couldn't save Rick. I knew that I'd watch him, bobbing out at sea, with my hands in hair and pace up and down in a panic, a true coward. So I grabbed a hold of Rick's arm.

'You're drunk, Rick,' I said. 'Don't do it.'

Rick tried to struggle free. I held him tighter. He looked at me, much like he had looked at that pint in Dio's earlier. 'Let go,' he moaned. 'Let go. I won't go. I won't. God's sake.'

I hung on for a while longer until Rick went completely limp and stared at me blankly. By the time I had let go of his arm the crowd had become bored and turned to finish their seaside snuff show. Rick gathered up his clothes and began to walk the last few yards back to the campsite entrance. I followed him a few steps behind.

At the campsite, Rick got dressed and then, still without speaking a word, began to pack up his tent. So I packed up mine too, the earth still spinning, but my mind sober.

When the commotion had died down around the rocks, we found the campsite owner's daughter and paid for our stay. She had been out all afternoon with her friends, so he hadn't seen the man drown, but she had heard about it from another camper. A lifeguard was apparently on his way to recover the body, she told us.

'It's very sad,' she said as she stuffed our Euros into her tight back pocket. 'Very sad. Did you see what happened?'

Rick shook his head. 'No,' he said. 'I only heard.'

She frowned for a moment, but then spotted the lifeguard in his yellow t-shirt and red shorts walking towards the beach and hurried over to him. We walked on up the road and waited at the coach stop on the edge of the town. It was a good time for us to move on and travel.

Clare Stewart

Past's Firearm

She used the firearm
        of her past
to kill her future.

Silvery seams of fears
        ran through her
Anxiety's glittering marble
        hardened her to possibility
        steeled her against hope.

John Humphreys

Song for sorrows

In hidden traces, in seams untracked,
the unglinting coal hides its diamonds.
In the upturned sky buried in the fault-lines,
clouds hide from their destiny.

Rained tears run in rivulets of days drowned,
gulps of sadness too strong to save breathing.

The wilting of nature's skin, the hollow
blackened stumps of trees, ringed evidence
of hours erased under an ugly moon, that lost
its light running for the pale cover of morning.
Blizzards of shadow hunted through shaking sound,
echoes of generations' hurt held heirlooms.

The wind whips and whispers the panic of leaves,
shouts its unknowing terror ground-wards to the
buried beneath fossils of frightened fantasy.

Unsow the sod, empty the grass of its grandeur,
groundling blades of grace ripped open, exposed
elemental electricity, haunting tundra, weeds of
waiting, worry-beads of the fumbled furrow,
seeds of longing.

Calcifying crows, caw songs for sorrows, coo rattle
and click their insanity to the blackened siren sun.
Winter undresses nature, bares all to the heathen
heavens in this nakedness of seasons, clinging cold
to all company, cruel companion corpse to Spring's
ambition. Bestial bride to the broken earth, rotted
flesh of frost-tide, hoary hoax of hope, mummifying
Mithra.

The drone of days bewitches sense, as barren bone
stands stripped of beauty. Unfleshed fruit decayed
in rotted romance.

The quieting notes coo lully lullay to the insistent
night.
Rattled skyward, the unhinged dance of midnight
comes home to collect its child as weeping stars fall
in this motherless nativity.

Juniper berried blood drinks the last drop of reason,
burying the bones deeper than the heart can fathom,
making murder of majesty, till the ancient tides
flow once more.

Ceiling of sky

Under a ceiling of sky
emptied of dreams,
he held the blackened duvet
come apart at the seams.
It spilled out monsters,
it avoided love,
it settled for a doorway,
a handout from a food truck.

Under a ceiling of stars
the night ran cold through his veins,
like the lost hope searching
for that midnight train.
Morning brought sunlight,
a breath too late,
a body in a doorway
that couldn't escape.

Let him ride easy, Lord let him roll,
he finally found that midnight train
carrying away his soul.

Love Song (for Kathleen)

You're the fog cracked 50's inner sleeve
You're the kiss of the needle on groove
You're the "well alright" expectation
You're the bass-line makes furniture move.

You're the cocaine crack in a broken voice
You're the midnight soft blues moan
You're the repeat match strike of a sunken scratch
You're the minor chords ransacking the home.

You're the goose honk of a bee-bop horn
You're the pineapple sweetness of an Hawaiian steel
You're the sunlight wanderings of a Jazz scat
You're the tap of a Cuban heel.

You're the souk of a Middle-Eastern raga
You're the ocean swell of an orchestra's strings
You're the angry snap of the ghetto
You're the blue notes sadness brings.

You're the thump of Brummie metal
You're the twisted stinging sitar
You're the glory hallelujah
You're the gently weeping guitar.

You're the Too Much Magic Bus

You're the In The Still Of The Night regret
You're the endless Good Vibrations
You're the Satisfaction I can get.

You're the music memory brings
You're the permanent mix-tape
You're the silent ending disc
You're the centre hole cancer made.

Anna Wall

when eyes and skies collide

we'd taken a walk to the edge of the world
curious as to it's limits.
a spinal column amidst the sheep shorn grass
bone beacon towards
rock teeth, ripe for climbing.
the sharp scratch of prehistory against shins
a timely reminder of mortality
and in the summit
waves and backwash tricked our eyes into creatures
a repetitive lull of fiction.
which is always more tempting
than the truth
that perhaps life is enough in the motion.

Cardiology

Scratch the surface again
curiosity pawing until the claws went in.
Pull it back.
Pull it back.
The red underneath,
chaos made flesh.

The push of desire,
the draw of death
all sits here
beneath the hinged ribs of wondering.

Emteaz Hussain

The Edge

she walks the edge of time and space
consciously suspect of the lies
that block her way
wanting the best in life
can be a drag
and has a price to pay
it could have made her hard and cold
and now she tries to soften the blow
the bruised internal
that's avoiding the maternal sacrifice
priding her self in her lonely search for truth
as she walks the edge of time and space

she feels she doesn't belong
as she searches for her place in the sun
a balancing act
between her fear of the oppressors
aware of the power she possesses
conscious of her every move
as she walks the edge of time and space

she gives a little of her heart
but holds on to her soul
selling her self is a game she plays
knowing her target before she aims
conscious of their every move
as she walks the edge of time and space

Born To Fight

I was born a daughter of a steel worker
Son of a farmer from a land in the East
Full of colour, spices, warmth and smells
Pain and hunger, fear and oppression

I was born a daughter of a steel worker
Baby of a mother with the name of Asha
Daughter of a farmer from a land in the East
And we were sewn and watered, fed and grown

And we struggled as we were moulded and formed
in the heat
Because I was born a daughter of a steel worker
And I kicked and I ran to face the night
With those hungry and those desperate searching
eyes

I faced reality in the homeless
And the shame of the rejected
And I ran and danced to face the night
And from the lightness and darkness
There formed a balance

Because I was born a daughter of a steel worker
And we were raised in the life of love and hope
Cos I was born the daughter of a steel worker

And the baby of a mother with the name of Asha

And I was raised in the light and
I was born to fight

Frank McMahon

Dr Who Childhood

Scarier than all the Daleks and all the Cybermen,
Were mom and dad arguing,
Or rather mom's sustained verbal attack
On dad.
She may as well have been screaming
"Exterminate!, exterminate!"
Hiding behind the sofa didn't make it go away.

One time they argued in the car
All the way to Wales.
I wanted to move in time and space,
Escape that confined place,
But I was only seven,
And not a Timelord,
With only one heart
And no Tardis.

Do Or Die Poets

Dog Called Bukowski – Tom Bailey

It's you with the dog called Bukowski
It's you I haven't met yet
It's me getting too close
It's you forgetting.

It's not that I don't want to
It's that I won't let me.
Truth is
There is an expiry date on my love
And our time together.

It's you with the dog called Bukowski
It's me with chronic detachment
It's as soon as you started chewing with your
    mouth open
It's your nipping, nagging and narcissistic behaviour
When I wanted to be alone.

It's me at the pub
Greeting both my friend and my enemy.

It's you with the dog called Bukowski
It's you not letting me take a piss while you shave
    your armpits.
It's you making fun
When they're around

Like you had to prove
This is a game
Where winner takes all.

Please do me one favour
And change that dogs name

Because its you
With the dog called Bukowski.

Enough – Ella Burns Robbins

You are not tall enough
Broad enough
Thin enough
Fat enough
You are not good enough

Pocket full of pintsized change
Colours fade
Fuzzy haze
Blinding white off a toilet seat
Steady now… Find your feet

You just want to *groove*
Slick kid on a Friday night
Couple more
Start a fight
Still not good enough

But you feel taller now
Broader somehow
Thin enough
Fat enough
Good enough

Your jaw slants to a frown
But your attention is not around

To notice the bloody nose
Stained sleeve, red smears across cheek bones

One too many?
Have a cheeky vomit
Soon enough you'll be back on it
Just won't remember where
you spent your last tenner

Down for days
Contemplating life
Trying your skin on for size

Make a change
Rinse your frame
Make meat obsolete from your diet
But don't acquire
Knowledge of what you really require

Fall asleep on your three-piece suit
Watch your smart TV
Do more
Eat less
Fit into that size 8 dress
Until you feel

Broad enough
Thin enough

Fat enough
Good enough

The Parents – Lolly Dean

They keep you safe, they keep you warm,
They offer you comfort, They give you a home.
If this is so simple and what parents do
My Mum and Dad missed those lessons at school

Too young, too scared, I was the grown one,
Fighting the bailiffs, being sister AND mum
It was a daily thing to hear them say,
Can somebody please take our children away.

My nan did her best, she often stepped in,
Feeding us, laundry, she did more than plenty.
The problem was that she couldn't admit,
Her beautiful son was now such a pig.

She never saw that two in the morning,
He and his friends came back drunk with no
warning.
Hitting, poking, pulling my hair
I must get up and cook for all that are there

As time went on, it was regular occurrence,
Got very apt at hiding bruised and tired appearance
My "job" I did well, my kid brother you see,
Hailed Dad as a hero and saw only how good he
could be

People often ask why I'm not bitter and angry,
It was a gift you see, gave me feeling and empathy
This is a story not for sadness or pity
But to say keep on fighting when things just seem shitty.

Poem –Tracy Shaw

<u>A</u>

A tiny bud of green slips its way into view;
slowly, but deliberately, life begins anew.
Nature does not falter if things don't go to plan;
she will just begin again if disrupted by man.

Does she have a secret power I can't understand,
to use when things get difficult, as if upon demand?
It seems so calm and practical,
design of simple brilliance;
complex tools of coping
just boil down to pure resilience.

<u>B</u>

Prism of light
...shafts so bright;
colours in rays stream across range of sight.
Shadows dancing to and fro;
dappled light ebbs in ….and then out it goes.
Arching branches sway in warm breeze;
leaves rustle as if chattering with a calm Sunday ease.
A stream softly babbles as it flows through my mind,
carrying away thoughts as I slowly unwind.

C

Sleep, curling whispy tendrils around my mind...
calming... relaxing muscles... lengthening breath.
Soothing away thoughts that I ...cant...
quite remember.
Solidarity becomes gradually translucent...
as cognition of my body recedes.
I float gently and surreally
into an unknown 'beyond'.

D

We purr.
A cosy sofa.
Fluffy pyjamas.
The Sunday feeling.

E

Open your mind;
explore paths to be defined.
Imagine possibility;
freedom from fragility.
Create and strengthen your resolve;
maybe feel a little bold!?
Seek a deeper truth,
held cocooned inside since youth.

Control finally taken,
untapped resources waken.
Move forward now, fresh and true,
Power at last claimed back by you!

Self Portrait - Charles Stickley

I remember the smell of elderflower
I don't remember before I was born
I have always read registration numbers
I have never learned to drive
I have been to the Bronx by mistake
I have never been to Margate
I have seen a thousand stars, Jupiter and Mars
I have never seen a live opera,
or a play by Harold Pinter
I always used to say I'll be an astronaut one day.

They always said to me you'll do brain surgery,
I know that I won't.
I don't know Lithuanian
I don't want to go back to Hull unnecessarily
I have always wanted a pet capybara.
I was always the kid who plays the piano
I was never the kid who paid attention at cricket
(except once, thank God)
I hate eating liver and being too hot
I love being by flowing water.

My favourite smell is freshly-picked basil
or coriander
My favourite feeling is being content, even euphoric
My worst feeling is best left behind.

I think I will feel better if I stick to the plan
I try hard to be in the moment
I try not to ruminate
The one thing I learned in school was
not to take anything at face value
The one thing I try to forget about school is
the food
My favourite thing in the world is
nature in all its forms
If I could avoid any fate it would be
an entry in the Darwin awards
If I could do anything in the world it would be
to see the Northern Lights
At the end of my life I would like to be able to say,
"Well, that was interesting!"

London Me – James Sinclair

London me was confident and always had a smile
He had time for all and would go the extra mile
He had no fear and troubles were few
He was successful, always knowing what to do

I'm not saying times were easy
Or anywhere near ideal
But He had the strength and support
To ensure He would "Keep It Real!"

Truth Is Final In A Political Cocktail
– Adrian Kelley

Trump when I was a kid meant fart
The Elgin Marbles is prize art
Greece and England still Worlds apart

Then we have Asad acting like Count Vlad
Whilst bezzie mate Putin sticks the boot in
Like a modern Rasputin

A POLITICAL NEWS BULLETIN
It's a fact, yes we're freezing
A new cold war is looming

Mugabe is fuming since someone
Took his place, not another disgrace?
Brexit means exit but sounds like a
biscuit

Kim Jong Un will risk it and fire one
Off toward the coast of Japan, they
Are annoyed one false move and we're
All destroyed

Angular rectangular Merkel, like a wise
Old turtle emerges from a political sea
To unbury diplomacy

If exploding radioactive bombs weren't
Enough, a pacific clown fish called Nemo
Swims into a supermarket plastic bag and drowns

Because our reality is stranger and more
Dangerous than fiction whilst fact and TRUTH
IS FINAL IN A POLITICAL COCKTAIL?

Alphabet Soup Poem – Beverley Jane Green

A is for an aeroplane flying in the sky
B is a baby who's unhappy and cries
C is a candle burning so bright
D is for darkening into the night
E is for energy that comes from within
F is for feelings some good and some bad
G is for garden that reminds me of my dad
H is for home of which I am glad
I is for isolation which happens to most
J is for July mostly warm and bright
K is for kindness that anyone can share
L is for listening to everyone who cares
M is for mountains so steep sometimes in pairs
N is for nationality, so many who cares
O is for orange we peel and eat
P is for plimsoles we put on our feet
Q is for Quavers some love to eat
R is for rain that falls from the sky
S is for summer which is mostly dry
T is for turning a new chapter in life
U is for understanding, a loving wife
V is for venus a planet somewhere
W is for window where we stand and peer
X is for x factor I love to watch
Y is for young ones who love to live and dance
Z is for a zoo that could start a romance